# Merry Christmas, Mom and Dad

Missi Magalis

HC
Happy Creek Publishing

My perception of the truth

Merry Christmas, Mom and Dad

Published by Happy Creek Publishing
Front Royal, VA 22630

Library of Congress Control Number: 2014957099

ISBN: 0989597466
ISBN-13: 978-0-9895974-6-3

For Mom and Dad

♥

## Acknowledgments

I couldn't have completed this project without a few very special
Santa's helpers.
Thank you, Brooke, Robin, Kerry Lane, and Kahle.

## Because of You

I know I've accomplished
greatness
because I married you.
I've been blessed with
perfection
because I gave birth to
You
 and
  You
   and
    You.
I know fame and fortune
joy, hope, faith, love
by looking into the eyes of
You
 and
  You
   and
    You
     and
      You.

MdM
13 March 2009

Merry Christmas,
Mom and Dad

Dear Reader,

What follows are some of my most precious Christmas memories. They are written in no specific order. As I remembered them, I wrote them down, counting backward from twenty-five—an advent calendar of sorts. Some memories, I realized were more vague than others, and I asked myself why. After re-reading the pages, I learned something rather unique about my memories: The pieces of my past I am able to recall most clearly are the imagery and emotions. The smells and sounds and the feelings of love and gratitude. The sense of family and togetherness and the lengths a mom and dad will go in order to provide some of the best childhood memories a girl could ask for.

If you're a parent, you know how difficult the holidays can be, the challenges of getting everything just right so those you love can look back with fondness on a day designed for peace and goodwill. Kids, I know you've been taught the important lessons of giving and gratitude, but I also know you're keeping your fingers crossed that Santa will bring everything on your list. I was young once too. Who am I kidding? I still love presents. My hope is that the memories in this book capture the true essence of Christmas from a parent's as well as a child's perspective.

I love Christmas. I love the warmth and peace giving brings, the love that is the reason for the desire to give in the first place. Christmas is a magical time I look forward to each year. This Christmas I've been blessed with the idea to write a book for my parents. A short but important one celebrating two people who did the best they could. A gift given freely—I never had to ask. They gave the best of themselves. Thank you, Mom and Dad.

❄

‹25› My earliest Christmas memory is of my grandfather on my mother's side. I called him Pappy. It was Christmas Eve, just after supper. I don't recall what I put on my plate that evening, probably because I was very young and likely because I was too excited for Santa's visit to even think about food at that particular moment.

My grandparents were over for supper, as was my uncle who'd visited from Ohio. Dad was at the table; Mom and my sister were doing the dishes. Me, I was flailing around the living room on a sugar high from too many cookies and a promise from Dad that I'd get to open one present before I went to bed. That's about the time I heard, "Ho, ho, ho," outside on the porch. Then a knock came at the door. I'm pretty sure I squealed so loud I about burst my nanny's eardrums.

I don't remember who answered the door, just that Santa appeared, a sack over his shoulder, his suit that bright shiny red, his hat slightly askew. Someone got him a chair from the kitchen. He sat down in the middle of the living room, rested his sack at his side, looked at me and smiled. My hands were clasped in front of me just under my chin as Santa leaned forward and motioned me to come closer. Not overly bashful, I inched forward until I was so close I could smell the aftershave on his skin. It was an awfully familiar scent.

I smiled at Santa as he lifted his gloved hand, tapped his cheek with his middle finger and said, "How 'bout a kiss right here, Misso?"

I unclasped my hands leaned in a little closer, took hold of his beard and pulled, revealing the imposter. "You are *not* Santa. You are Pappy!"

I remember Pappy laughing and sitting back in his chair. I don't know if he changed out of the suit or kept it on, or what was in the sack he brought. I don't recall feeling a loss of innocence at having realized the real Santa hadn't come calling. In fact, I continued believing in Santa after that night. Probably, my mother made up a great tale about how the real Santa would be along after I was asleep, that Pappy was pretending like the Santas did in the mall. Whatever she came up with, it worked, because I do not recall being scarred by this occasion. What I do remember is the supreme satisfaction of recognizing Pappy behind that beard and, most importantly, the sound of my parents laughing.

✻

◀24▶ Christmas Eve has always been special to me. Every year of my childhood, this day was just about the same in a number of ways, but it was never boring. It was the routine that I welcomed. I knew that my parents would be off work, that Mom would spend the day cooking, and Dad would be itching for evening.

Dad was like a kid at Christmas, always wanting to give early presents. If I'm not mistaken, it was his idea for us to open one present on Christmas Eve. It could've been that Mom suggested it when she saw just how excited he was during the holidays. Whoever decided that a Christmas Eve present was in order, I'm thrilled. It's a tradition I've carried into my adult life. What's funny is that my sister and I got the same thing on Christmas Eve every single year. Still, I'd tear the paper off the box and pull off the top, rip through the tissue paper like I had no idea a new pair of pajamas was inside.

No matter how scratchy or how much store smell lingered, I wore my new pajamas to bed. They added to the excitement of the presents that would be under the tree the next morning. This made it hard to get to sleep. Some years, if I absolutely could not get myself to be still and close my eyes, my sister would allow me to go to her room.

One year stands out in my mind like it was yesterday. My sister let me bring my pillow, stuffed rabbit, and blanket to her bed. I was elated to be in her room. She is eight years older than me, and, back then, I'd have done just about anything to go in her room and be near her stuff. She had so many records and this big comb and a hairbrush and high heel shoes and a fuzzy robe and a purple baseball hat with silver wings. God, how I just wanted to grab hold of all of it—play her records, comb my hair, wrap myself up in that warm robe and dance like I was one of those women on the front of her records. I'd done this on occasion and gotten whacked in the head for it. So, it'd have to be enough on Christmas Eve that I got to be *near* all of it. I knew I wouldn't be able to do anything other than lie stiff as a board in her bed, but that didn't matter. I was getting something better than what I got when I slipped into her room when the coast was clear. I was getting to be with my big sister.

She tried to be patient. Talked to me about what I wanted for Christmas, hoping I'd get tired and fall asleep. But talking about what I wanted only made me that much more excited. Finally, she told me I had to go to sleep or Santa would never leave the presents. That didn't work either. The quiet made me wriggle around like I had ants in my pants. I thought my sister might whop me a good one.

That night, however, she did not lose her patience. Instead, she fabricated this great plan. Told me if I turned my pillow sideways and laid on top of it, that I would go to sleep. She said she'd done it before and that it worked for her.

Anxious for Santa to come, I did exactly as she said. I turned my pillow sideways and curled up tight on the standard sized pillow. I stayed real still and waited. And waited and waited and waited. Eventually, I must've drifted off because the next time I opened my eyes it was 4:30 in the morning. I pushed on my sister. Nudged and poked, told her it was Christmas and time to get up.

I believe, at sixteen, my sister would've liked to have Christmas a little later. But, she did what big sisters do; she got out of bed. I don't believe she said, "Merry Christmas" or anything. I was only eight at the time. I'm sure I probably thought everyone should be excited to be up and opening presents so early. Looking back, I'm certain my sister could not wait to go back to bed.

This is another year I have no idea what I got for Christmas. What I remember is having a big sister who found a way to get me to go to sleep on Christmas Eve and, even though she didn't want to, she got up without complaining just a few hours later.

❄

◀23▶ Every Christmas Eve after supper and after Nanny and Pappy left for home two blocks away, Dad would drive Mom, me, and my sister around town to look at Christmas lights. Dad would go out and warm up the car while we got ready. For me, getting ready meant throwing a blanket or coat on over my new pajamas (or old ones if we hadn't opened our Christmas Eve present yet). For Mom, it meant throwing on shoes and grabbing her purse. For my sister, it likely meant combing her hair and primping just in case she saw someone she knew while we were sitting at a stop light.

When I was growing up, there seemed to be more colored lights than white. A whole lot of nativity scenes. Definitely no hanging icicle lights. And none of the blow up decorations that dot people's yards today. Just lots and lots of colored lights and plastic candles, Santas, and snowmen. I guess some might think of today's blow-up decorations as plastic decorations evolved. I think whoever dreamed up blow-up decorations should have left well enough alone. You will never convince me that anything is prettier than the decorations I grew up with. That includes the silver tree we had. You know, the one where the silver branches are so sparse you can see the matching silver pole running up the middle. The best decorations for this tree were either colored balls or blue ones, definitely blue lights, and a white felt skirt to hide the stand (as if the stand is what made the whole thing look fake).

While my parents enjoyed touring the town to look at the lights, I believe they had another motive as well. My guess is they thought if they got the car really toasty warm

I'd get super tired and be ready for bed when we got home. But their plan was flawed (if this was their plan at all). I do recall getting drowsy in the car, but when we pulled in the driveway at home, no matter how tired I'd become, the excitement returned as soon as my cheeks felt the cold winter air. I'd breathe in that clean crisp scent, the one that smells like Christmas and snow, and I'd be wide-awake. I'd bound inside, and, if we hadn't opened our one present, I'd ask if we could. If we had, I went straight for the cookies to stuff myself even fuller than I'm sure I already was.

If Mom and Dad were tired after such a long day, I never knew. Years later, I'd come to appreciate their efforts to make our Christmas bright. It wasn't until I became a mother that I understood this holiday means even less sleep for the adults than it does for the excited munchkins waiting to hear reindeer hooves on the roof.

But, I do remember someone else whose eyes popped open often before mine. Tired or not, Dad was just as big a kid as I was on Christmas morning. Mom, who I'm sure had to be exhausted from all the cooking, cleaning, and wrapping, would slip on her blue fuzzy robe, tie the belt, and say, "Merry Christmas." She'd pour a cup of coffee to wake herself up while Dad lit a fire in the basement. I'd have long since wakened my sister. She'd stand with me at the top of the steps, waiting.

I'd holler down, "Can we come down yet?"

"I'll let you know," Dad would yell back.

I always knew when I heard the crackling of the wood, smelled the burning paper and logs, felt the heat creeping up the stairs, that the time was growing ever nearer.

"Is it time yet?" I'd ask again. Mom would be sipping coffee by now, getting anxious herself. Though at the time I thought her anticipation was to see what Santa had left, I know now it was because she knew exactly what awaited, and she couldn't wait for our reaction.

"Well, what are you waiting for?" Dad would finally holler up as if we were the ones holding up the show. I'd nearly fall head over heels racing down those stairs. There was always a present that wasn't wrapped: a chalkboard one year, a red record player with flashing colored lights another. I recall getting a black Huffy bike, a chemistry set, Sneezy Baby, a toy grocery cart. I got a set of phones one year. One went in the kitchen, the other in my room. I could call Mom whenever I wanted. I called her so much the first few days, the phones soon disappeared, never to return. I don't remember being upset about it. Mom must've come up with a good story. If we'd had a garbage disposal, I'm sure the phones would've ended up in it. At any rate, I'm sure Santa chose his presents more carefully after that.

❄

‹22› I've already mentioned the silver tree we had upstairs. It was eventually replaced with a small green one. Fake, of course. Real ones were too much of a mess, Mom said. Plus, my sister and I had allergies. "You'd sneeze your heads off," Mom always said when I asked if we could get a real tree. I didn't believe her when she said this. I thought it was all because of that first excuse, the one about the needles. One thing my mother loathed was a mess. My room was never allowed to look like a cyclone hit it. If it did, I was not to come out until it was fixed.

Years later, I'd try a real tree in my own home. My husband and I went out, he chopped the thing down, brought it home, got it in the house all set up in its bucket of water. Within the hour, I was sneezing my head off. My husband carried it out to the truck and drove it away while I stayed behind and cleaned up the terrible mess. So, Mom had been right on both accounts, and I haven't had a real tree since.

I take that back. I salvaged one little Charlie Brown tree from behind a dumpster at a school. A teacher must've taken it down before Christmas break. I put it in the back of my car and took it home, set it up downstairs. My youngest daughter helped me decorate it. We stood back and admired our good find. I thought perhaps I'd outgrown my allergy. I wasn't sneezing *too* much. The tree was small; it didn't have a ton of needles, so, very little mess. "Perfect," I said out loud. But, I'd spoken too soon. My daughter began hacking and coughing. Needless to say, the tree was quickly deposited at the curb.

❄

◄21► Growing up, the big tree was always in the basement. We put it up the first week in December. Most years there were colored lights. As I said before, white lights didn't become popular until I was older. We always had matching balls and garland. Mom liked bows. We had these red velvet ones with gold around the middle. These were Mom's favorite ornament, I think. She messed with them for a really long time, anyway. She'd straighten and smooth the things long after I thought they looked just fine.

The upstairs tree was less formal. The bows were crocheted—some red, some white to match the candy canes that hung from the branches. The candy canes were magical. They disappeared. You probably don't have to think very hard to figure out where they went ... I ate them.

❄

◀20▶ It took a long time for me to understand the sacrifices my parents made to give my sister and me a good Christmas. They were very hard workers. Mom was a bookkeeper. Dad worked at Avtex for, gosh, I guess about eighteen years. They worked Monday through Friday. Mom worked nine until five; Dad went to work really early and got home around four. He also umpired and refereed ball games for extra money. Sometimes he'd have to go away for entire weekends to work tournament games. Mom and Dad kept the house warm and food on the table. I never recall wanting for anything, but that didn't mean it was always easy providing for a family of four.

Mom started planning for Christmas early. I know this because she started paying on Kmart and Zayre layaways not long after a new school year started, close to the time the leaves began changing. At the time, I didn't think anything of it. Now I understand how difficult this must've been. She'd have had to determine the right clothes size based on how much she thought we'd grow and decide what toys I'd ask for before there was even a list. My sister was older, wiser. She asked for the stuff she wanted before Mom went layaway shopping. I, on the other hand, would add to my list until the very last minute. I thought the layaway consisted of presents from Mom and Dad. I believed in Santa, which meant he could make anything I wanted in a flash.

I'd learn it was Dad who took care of these last minute additions to my list. These were the gifts that appeared under the tree after Mom warned I might not get every single thing on my list.

I'm not sure I always got everything on my list, but if I didn't it wasn't because my parents didn't try. Now, you might think this was terrible, that children are supposed to know up front that Santa might not bring it all, but I grew up in a house where we didn't get a ton of stuff throughout the year. We got clothes and shoes as we needed them, but the wants, the things we wished for, they came on birthdays and Christmas. Especially Christmas. This holiday has always been Mom and Dad's favorite, even during the rough patches life presented. We always, and I do mean always, had a nice Christmas no matter what else was going on. But it wasn't the presents that meant nearly as much as the love that went into the giving. The giving is the priceless part, the piece that made every bow a blessing and every box a treasure.

❄

◄19► Every Saturday after we finished cleaning, Mom, my sister, and I would climb in the car and ride to Winchester. My mom and sister loved, I mean absolutely adored, shopping. Me, I hated it. I was given a firm talking to about being on my best behavior before we ever left the house, another talk on the way, and one more before we entered the mall.

I have to say, I deserved every single warning. I was bad. Well, not bad really. Just rambunctious. I ran around a lot, made noises, got lost, hid in the clothes racks. Mostly, while I was wandering off or hiding, I was pretending something. I had to in order to survive. Shopping was the most horrid experience I wouldn't have wished on my worst enemy. For the most part, I still feel the same way. The occasional trip to Hagerstown to Christmas shop is fun. Actually, Christmas shopping anywhere can be enjoyable *sometimes*. The stars have to be aligned just right for my shopping genes to get excited. I'm telling you, folks, shopping just isn't my thing.

To get me to be good, Mom often bribed me. "I'll get you a cookie and milk from the cookie shop," she'd say.

My taste buds nearly hopped off my tongue every time she said it, but this particular bribe wasn't the one I yearned for. The one I would absolutely try my hardest to be good for. It wasn't until I heard the next bribe that I would quell my desire to run for the clothes racks. "And," she'd say, "if you are really good ..." It was always right around this part of the sentence that I started bouncing and had to stop myself so I wouldn't ruin my chances before the sentence was even out of her mouth. "I will get you a book."

Nine times out of ten, I tried and failed at being good. I was usually in another department hiding in the clothes within the first hour. But, if I got to Mom before she called out for me too many times, and if I looked super apologetic, I still got my treats.

You may think Mom was a pushover for caving, but I have to argue in her defense. First of all, I was on my personal best behavior and she knew it. To ask more of me would have meant trading me in for another kid. And two, Mom knew if she filled my belly I'd sleep the whole way home. She also knew if she got me a book I'd stay out of her hair for at least two days. If you ask me, this was smart thinking on her part.

I have to say, she got her money's worth. I still have all those books she got me from Waldenbooks in Apple Blossom Mall. And, though it's a rare occasion, whenever I walk into that mall, I am reminded of the bookstore and the many hours of joy that came from shopping there.

Memories. That's what this book is about. Not all of the memories I keep stored inside are good ones, but certainly the bad are not worth detailing. But mention them I will, because I don't want to give a false impression that everything in our world was hunky dory. Our family, like most everyone else's had its share of trouble. In fact, we had a lot of troubles, which makes this book even more valuable. Here's why: Even though we weren't the Perfects, and by Perfects I mean Mr. and Mrs. Perfect and their adorable Perfect children—you know the type, the Cleavers and the Bradys are the two most popular, I think—even though we weren't anything like them, I can promise you this: my parents love for my sister and I was just as strong, if not stronger, than the love Mr. and Mrs. Perfect felt for their kids. I know this despite the troubles. How? All I have to do is think of Christmas and their feelings for us are more than clear.

I've already kind of sort of hinted that we weren't rich. But money isn't everything, and we managed. I guess I should say my parents managed. They were the ones who very rarely let us know when times were tough. Honestly, I can count only a few occasions when I got an inkling that money was an issue. It wasn't until my parents divorced that I really considered money at all. I mean, I knew we had to have it to survive. Mom used to sit at the kitchen table once a month, write out checks, then ask if I wanted to ride with her while she drove all over town after dark placing this envelope in this night box and that envelope in another.

But, money wasn't the only issue, and after twenty few years, Mom and Dad decided they couldn't make their marriage work. And I was glad. The troubles of which I mention affected my sister and me too. Something had to give, and, I have to say, I'm glad it was their vows.

The purpose of this book is not to rehash the bad, but I feel it's necessary to paint an accurate picture, and it makes for a nice lead in to my next topic—two of the best Christmas presents I ever got. Neither were presented on Christmas Eve or even Christmas day. Both came into my life at different times, but I have to say, over the years, I've come to appreciate and cherish them more than any present under a tree. But then, people are always more important than things. The two people I'm writing about are more than precious to me. They are my stepparents.

My parents got lucky the second time around, which means I got lucky too. Not too long ago, Dad mentioned something about mistakes he'd made, and I was quick to respond. "If you hadn't made those mistakes, I wouldn't ever have gotten Betsy or Bobby."

Years ago, before I knew of the treasures that would come out of the turmoil, I was angry and uncertain and I asked, "Why me?" a whole lot. I'm not saying I was upset over my parents splitting up. I wholeheartedly agreed with their decision, but everything that made me want them apart had me wondering if any good could come of such pain. My stepparents are proof that silver linings absolutely exist. Beyond the shadow of a doubt.

❄

◄18► I mentioned earlier that Christmas is the reason I know my parents loved my sister and me. I don't mean that I didn't feel their love at any other time of the year. What I mean is I knew it *especially* during this holiday.

For two days, a complete forty-eight hours, my parents were different. It was like they made a pact that nothing else mattered but family and happiness for these two days. The house was filled with the scent of baking cookies, Nanny brought a fruitcake, Dad watched television and occasionally stole cookies meant for later. I ate the cookie dough *and* the cookies. Except the peanut butter ones—I only ate the kiss off of these. If Mom caught me stealing the chocolate off the top, I got in trouble, but there were times I was successful. I'd pick up a cookie, sit at the table and pretend to eat it. I'd pluck the kiss off the top, crumble the rest and put it in the lip of metal band that decorated the edge of the kitchen table. Mom must've found it because it was always gone when I checked, but she never said anything. She saved the scolding for the times she caught me in the act.

Most years we went to the Christmas Eve service at church. Seems we went to church a lot in December, I guess because of all the extra services. Nanny sang in the cantata and I was in the Christmas play. I remember being an angel a couple different years. One year, I held the baby, so I must've gotten to be Mary. I remember always wanting to be Mary but someone else usually got to be her. Funny how the year I was probably her, I don't even remember the complete experience. All I recall is holding the plastic doll that represented baby Jesus.

❄

◄17► Most always, presents came from Mom and Dad or Ho Ho. Growing up, I remember two presents that came from just Dad all by himself, only one of which he took credit for on the tag.

One of the late in the game presents I asked for one year just happened to be what every other girl in the world wanted: a cabbage patch doll. Mom was pretty sure this wasn't going to happen. And said as much. For real. Her, "I don't think so," was serious. It came with a frown that said, "I mean it."

But, one evening a few days before Christmas, my dad called to talk to Mom. I heard her on the phone asking how much. Then she said, "Are you sure?"

Later, years later, I'd find out that conversation was about Hettie Camelia, the cheerleader cabbage patch doll I still have at age forty-one. Mom wasn't sure they could swing the cost of the doll. Being a hot new item, they were incredibly expensive. Mom had already finished Christmas shopping which meant the holiday budget had been depleted. I don't know how, but Dad made my wish come true. On Christmas morning, I got my doll. The tag read: From Ho Ho.

This was one of Dad's favorite ways of showing love. Sacrificing the little he had and coming through with something someone else may have thought impossible. I am his kid which meant I was worth it.

Note to Dad: I appreciate the doll. Most of all I am grateful for the reason behind the gift—your love. But I'd have known you loved me even if you hadn't gotten me that doll. I knew when you hugged me and when you told me you loved me that I was a reason for you to live. And that's still true today.

The other present Dad got me on his own came during one of the more tense times in our home. Christmas was still sacred though. Thankfully, the two day truce remained intact. Everything went as planned for Christmas Eve complete with a visit from Santa perched on top of a fire truck, shouting, "Ho Ho Ho" as he threw bags of candy to the kids waving excitedly from the curb. On Christmas morning, Mom still made pancakes in the shape of gingerbread men for me. The house still smelled of bacon and butter and syrup. We still had ham for Christmas dinner. But there was an unspoken tension that everyone could feel.

The only way I am certain of this tension is because I connect it with the only other odd occurrence. A gift for me just from Dad—a doll dressed in a patchwork dress and hat that plays "Santa Claus is Coming to Town." I still have the doll, still wind it occasionally and watch her twirl as the song plays. And I still wonder what made Dad buy this doll. I love it, of course, and I was excited to receive it. But the gift itself has always been a mystery to me because, until then, Mom and Dad had never done separate shopping for my sister and me. That was the only time I ever remember it happening when I was young.

Looking back, I think perhaps this gift was a sign of things to come. A sign of my parents' separateness, of their independence, of their freedom from one another. To me, that doll was a symbol of change.

✵

<16> It would be neglectful of me if I failed to mention two important women in these pages. Both loved me unconditionally, thought I was fabulous, and I felt the same way about them. My grandmothers.

Nanny lived close-by, only two streets over. I believe I've already mentioned this. I saw Nanny on every holiday right up until she and Pappy moved to Florida. I was almost a teenager when they moved, not too long after the Christmas I got that musical doll from Dad. Just another sign that life is more about change than it is about staying the way it was when I was a kid. I guess change is what makes memories so precious. It's the images, the scents, the sounds, the songs and words and textures that help remind us of the moments that are dear to us.

Grandma, my dad's mom, lived in Pennsylvania. I only saw her half a dozen times or so a year, and rarely on Christmas. In fact, I only remember one Christmas she visited, and it wasn't actually Christmas day. She arrived in a station wagon along with a few other family members. She carried with her a white bag full of gifts that she emptied under our small upstairs tree. I about wiggled myself to death when she did this because it could only mean one thing: that I'd get to tear into a present or two before Christmas Eve even. And I was right, but for the life of me I can't remember what I got. What I do remember is Grandma's face as she watched me sitting in the middle of the floor playing with whatever it was she brought me. It's like a snapshot in my mind, and it's as clear as if it were yesterday—when I looked up, I saw Grandma sitting on the edge of our gold and cream couch. She didn't look uncomfortable, but I remember thinking she might feel better if she would sit back and relax into the cushions. One hand was fisted on her hip, the other gripped the arm of the couch. Her elbow did not rest on the arm. She held it up in the air. Her face was the color of a caramel candy—a sharp contrast against the bright green brown eyes that reminded me of looking up from a forest floor into the tree canopy. She was lovely. Especially when she smiled. And this was just what she was doing when I looked up from the floor that day. Her eyes crinkled at the corners so that tiny lines spider-webbed to her temples, and her lips formed a perfect crescent moon that lifted her cheeks and held them there like two perfect planets. Her eyes, they were forest stars, shining just for me. And what I saw that I carry with me to this day was her love for me.

❄

◀15▶ Every year Nanny made a fruitcake for Christmas. And she insisted I have a slice. I only sort of loved Nanny's fruitcake. If she'd just left out the dang walnuts, the thing would've been just fine, but she had to add the nasty things. My youthful taste buds were not a fan. I've gotten better about walnuts. I can at least tolerate them now (not the dark ones—they are still disgusting), but back then, when she asked me to try her fruitcake I was constantly trying to figure out a way to work around those nuts.

I tried digging them out when she wasn't looking, but I could never get them all. Nanny chopped the nuts so small they were everywhere, like tiny hard-shelled bugs. I'd bite into one and its guts would explode that bitter taste on my tongue. I hated those nuts. They were the perfect ingredient to keep me out of the fruitcake. This went for cookies too. I think it should be a rule that any cake or cookie made for the Christmas holiday should absolutely *not* have nuts in it. Again, I'm a little more tolerant of the nuts now that I'm older, but back then they were the devil trying to ruin Christ's birthday.

Still, there were parts of Nanny's fruitcake that were good. The flavor of the cake itself was spicy and sweet. Sort of cinnamoney. The raisins were good, but I got those for snack all the time, so they didn't really impress me all that much. The candied cherries were, by far, the best part of the cake. So, here's how I got through a slice of it:

Like I said, I'd wait for Nanny to turn her back, then I'd work frantically to get as many of the bugs out as possible. I have no idea where I put them, possibly on the floor. Then I'd dig out the raisins and eat those. The candied cherries came next. They were the best. Then I'd dip the cake into a cup of milk Nanny gave me, and pray to God I didn't bite into a well-camouflaged walnut.

Once my vocabulary grew, I was able to describe a slab of Nanny's fruitcake perfectly … dense. The thing was dense. No matter how you cut it dissected it chewed it, those cake ingredients managed to find their way back together right in the pit of the stomach. I imagine the cake rebuilding itself in perfect form, insisting on making its way through the intestines whole.

But … it *was* good. Really, it was. In recent years, my uncle has taken up the fruitcake baking tradition. I have a taste just so I can draw forth a precious memory of Nanny. I feel her presence in the flavors and textures. And I am reminded of the sacrifice she made to create it—the hard work and money that went into it. In case you didn't know, fruitcakes are expensive to make and a lot of work to get just right. At least, that's what I've been told over the years.

Apparently, Nanny's was perfect every single time. Despite the walnuts, I think this is true. Nanny was a great baker, so I'm sure her fruitcake was the best out there. If she'd just left out those nuts!

❄

◀14▶ As long as we're on the subject of my lovely nanny, I may as well share another memory that may sound a tad familiar to those of you who've read some of my earlier work. A memory that taught me to listen to my inner voice when it tells me I'm on the wrong path.

The particular path to which I am referring here is a skinny staircase to the attic, each step taking me closer to my big Christmas present. See, for some reason Nanny got it in her head that she wanted to share Christmas with me early. Out of the blue she asked if I'd like to see one of my presents. At first, I hesitated, but the excitement that lit up her face soon had me saying yes. I have to clarify something before I go on. I was not ever a present snooper. I have always loved the anticipation leading up to Christmas morning. But, for whatever reason, I guess the glow on Nanny's sweet face, I followed her up those stairs and saw … Sneezy Baby.

Golly, was she beautiful. She had blond hair and blue eyes, a short-sleeved white dress with tiny blue flowers and eyelet edging. And, best of all, when you squeezed her stomach, she let out a sneeze. I'd asked for this doll, put her on my list for Ho Ho. I'd prayed for her, yearned for her, and for one second, I was overwhelmed with joy that I was getting the very present I asked for. But, when I turned away from the box that held my doll, followed Nanny back down the stairs, my joy was replaced with an emptiness that made me so very sad.

It didn't take long at all for Mom to find out. I can't remember if I told her right away or if she dragged it out of me later when my solemn mood didn't lighten. I was down in the dumps for several days. Every time I thought of Sneezy, I wished I could un-think her.

Mom was furious when she learned what had happened. I remember Mom flying into Nanny with both feet. I heard snippets of the recount, how Nanny had ruined my Christmas, showed me my big present, and Mom couldn't figure out why.

Nanny was remorseful. She was down in the mouth as long as I was down in the dumps. I just couldn't stand the tension all this caused. So, I did the only thing a kid could do. I pretended it didn't happen. I told myself I hadn't seen Sneezy Baby until I almost believed it. I told Mom and Nanny I didn't remember what was in the attic, that my big Christmas present couldn't be ruined if I couldn't remember what it was.

As an adult, I am completely aware that Nanny and Mom were not fooled by my proclamation, but, at the time, it made me feel tons better. I'd fixed the problem, and on Christmas morning I acted super surprised and ecstatic when I opened the box with Sneezy Baby inside.

Only one problem presented itself that I couldn't fix in my mind after that Christmas. If Sneezy Baby was supposed to be my big present, that meant she should've been from Ho Ho. This could only mean that Ho Ho was really Mom and Dad.

For years, I told myself this couldn't be true, that Ho Ho is real. Today, I can say for sure, he is as real as all my hope and faith and heart will allow. And I have a whole lot of all three.

❄

◄13► What I'm about to write down could be a birthday memory. I can't be sure. The gift was either given to me a few days before my birthday or just before Christmas. I was fifteen, and my parents had recently separated. Mom and I were living in a tiny basement efficiency apartment. It was a clean, cozy little place to start over, but it wasn't easy. My mom had two jobs, working nine until five as a bookkeeper and five hours a night as a cashier at a grocery store. She rarely had a day off.

One Saturday, she cleared her schedule because Nanny and Pappy were coming to visit. They'd moved back from Florida to Maryland, still a few hours away, so we didn't get to see them as often as I'd have liked, but at least the visits were more frequent.

I do not recall Nanny and Pappy arriving or how we spent the day. Like many of the other memories in this book, I have a snapshot image of the moment, along with a snippet of conversation, that reminds me of the incredible understanding and forethought my nanny had.

Nanny was resting on the couch and I was walking in from the kitchen when she gave me the gift. It wasn't wrapped. In fact, it was sitting out as a decoration. I don't know when she put it in front of the fireplace hearth. For all I know I could've passed it throughout the day, but I think I would've noticed it. Though I would've had difficulty thinking it something for me or Mom.

"That's for you," Nanny told me, pointing to a ceramic Dalmatian. I didn't understand. The dog was beautiful, but it was a present I thought was more for an adult. Still, it wouldn't have been for Mom. She was never close to the Dalmatian we had when I was little. I was the one who was devastated when we couldn't keep Nishka. That dog loved me so much. She'd stretch out alongside me on my twin bed. I'd place her paws around my neck, and we'd both fall asleep that way. But, Nishka was always getting out and running away, so my parents got rid of her. I was heartbroken. Dad actually went back to get her the next day, but he came home without her. He said she'd died from heartworm. I never believed that. I always thought she died because she missed me.

Nanny loved Nishka as much as I did, which, I believe, is one of the reasons she gave me that ceramic dog. I believe Nanny knew her cancer was beginning to win, and she didn't want to wait to give me that present. She made the decision to give me a gift she'd have rather gotten years later if she'd had that kind of time left. But she didn't and she knew it, so she gave me the Dalmatian with a simple message: "You'll appreciate it someday."

I thanked her, told her I loved it. This was the truth. I told her I appreciated the dog already, and I thought I did. I couldn't understand why she'd used the word *someday*. Had I made a face that caused her to think I didn't like the gift? Did she see the few seconds of confusion when I looked around the hearth for something other than the dog?

I was in my twenties decorating my own home before I finally understood why Nanny had said, "You'll appreciate it someday." In choosing the perfect spot to display the Dalmatian, I thought about the double memory of him: my childhood dog, Nishka, and my nanny, who loved me so much she gave me a forever gift before I knew how much it would mean.

I still have the ceramic Dalmatian. It sits on our hearth in the living room. It has a few chips here and there, has had its paw snapped off a time or two, but it's been with me all these years, and I cherish it. Nanny was right—my appreciation is so much deeper than it was the day she gave it to me.

❄

◄12► Nanny once got me a subscription to *Pockets*, a kid's magazine with stories and activities in it. I looked forward to getting one each month. I'd get the mail out of the box, and when my magazine was among the envelopes, I'd carry it with me down to the basement, flop on the couch and read the thing cover to cover.

My favorite *Pockets* magazine was the Christmas one. It had an advent calendar in it. I opened a window each day, counting down to the greatest day of the year. But, the excitement over my new Christmas *Pockets* was overshadowed that year by the possibility of a bad grade in science. I would've done just about anything to avoid a bad grade. I didn't want to get grounded, and I didn't want to disappoint my parents. Especially not during the time of year when everything was good for a couple days. If I ruined the two best days of the year, I'd never forgive myself.

I don't recall being grounded or ruining Christmas, but I do remember a huge sense of relief just before winter break, so I must've brought the grade up. I'll never forget the sick worry in the pit of my stomach while I waited for that report card or the relief that meant Christmas was not going to go down the tubes because of me. The lights that year, I'm sure, were brighter, the wrapping paper extra shiny, the dinners and cookies extra flavorful, and all because I didn't let my parents down.

P.S. Along with the ceramic Dalmatian I've had all these years, I still have the *Pockets* magazines too.

❄

◁11▷ By the time my parents divorced, my sister was already married and living in her own home. It was a difficult period in all of our lives, especially financially. If I hadn't known much about making a dollar stretch before, I certainly knew it when my mom was working two jobs to keep us afloat.

Christmas in the apartment on Blue Ridge Avenue that year was not easy. I was older, and the traditions were changing as a result, but they were also a lot different because of our circumstances. The two day truce was off. Christmas Eve dinner that year … I have no idea if we had one. We probably went to my sister's. Our house wasn't filled with the scent of cookies in the oven; Mom worked too many hours and just didn't have time to do anything extra. And there was the money to consider. The bills had to be paid and we had to have food. I am sure chocolate chips were the last thing on the list and had to be crossed off because the necessities totaled more than the amount she budgeted.

What I did get that Christmas was yet another lesson in giving. That lesson came from my sister and brother-in-law. On Christmas morning I opened a new stereo that had a cd player in it. I got a Bon Jovi cd I'd asked for. And, I also got my high school class ring. My sister and her husband made Christmas happen for me that year. They wanted Mom take the credit, but pride wouldn't let her do that. She confessed before the sun set on Christmas day.

Something else I didn't miss was how Mom filled out the tags. Even though I was beyond believing in the man we called Ho Ho, she still filled in his name beside the word, From. Like Mom, I fill in the tags the same way even though my own children are grown because, after all, it's the hope we believe in, the faith that there is good in this world, that something larger than ourselves is looking out for our best interest. That's what the man in the red hat means to me, anyway. And he showed all the hope, faith, and goodness that year in the willingness of a young married couple to help our mother.

This act of kindness showed me something else, as well. In all of the turmoil and pain our family went through, Mom and Dad raised my sister and me to be kind and giving, to help others in need.

❄

◄10► Boy, was I glad when we moved into a townhouse, and not because I hated the apartment. I was elated because Mom was happier than I'd seen her in a while. We had our own rooms, she was in a better place financially and able to quit her second job, and she'd started dating the man who would become my stepfather.

Finally, Mom could rest in the evenings. She could breathe again. And at Christmas, she had time to bake cookies and make fudge. I'm pretty sure she used the chocolate chip cookie recipe on the back of the Nestle chip bag. No matter how many people use this recipe, a more perfect cookie never existed than the ones my mother pulled from the oven, the ones she'd mixed to perfection and dropped in perfectly measured rounded spoonfuls every single time. I love to bake but have never been able to master the skill of making the same size cookie every single time. Mom can make them look identical.

I think Mom got her fudge recipe from Nanny. Like the cookies, the same fudge recipe can be tried by many, but the successes are few. Not everyone has the magic touch it takes to get the creamy chocolate goodness just right. Believe me, I know. My own fudge, though usually very good, can sometimes turn out a mess. I haven't figured out what it is I do to create the bad batch, but I always blame the weather. Sounds like a good enough excuse to me.

A few years ago, Mom gave my sister and me a recipe book filled with copies of recipes from our nanny's collection. One of those recipes just happened to be my nanny's famous 2-Flavor Fudge. I used the recipe for the first time on December 12, 2013, (I know this because I made a note on the recipe.) and, for some crazy reason, I used substitutions. I must have been out of my mind to mess with what was already the very best (with the exception of the nuts she put in it). Maybe I got too confident, thought I could perfect what was almost flawless to begin with. After that attempt, I don't believe I've used this recipe since. It was good enough, but it wasn't like theirs (no idea why I thought it would be, what with the substitutions). Anyway, I stick with the recipe on the back of the marshmallow fudge container.

As I've already mentioned, the recipe Mom used calls for walnuts. This is one of the ingredients I didn't add the year I made it. I didn't want to have to suck the chocolate off and spit the walnuts in the trash like watermelon seeds. Still, Mom's fudge was delicious. You know it had to be good if I was willing to work around those nuts!

As a merry Christmas to anyone who happens to read these pages, I will record the 2-Flavor Fudge recipe for you. If you have children, hopefully they like walnuts.

# 2-Flavor Fudge

Combine in saucepan, 2 cups firmly packed brown sugar, 1 cup granulated sugar, 1 cup evaporated milk, ½ cup butter or margarine. Bring to *full boil* over moderate heat, stirring frequently. Boil for 15 minutes, over moderate heat, stirring occasionally. Remove from heat. Add 1 jar marshmallow cream (5-oz. to 10-oz. jar), one 6-oz. package each Nestle's Butterscotch and Semi-Sweet Chocolate Morsels; stir till Morsels are melted and mixture is smooth. Blend in 1 cup Diamond Walnuts, chopped, and 1 tsp. vanilla. Pour into greased 9-inch square pan. Chill until firm. Yield: about 2 ½ pounds.

*Note: I do not know if the brand makes a difference, but considering the fact that I've tried substitutions before and made a mess of things, I'm not willing to take any chances this time around. I don't want to steer you wrong either, so I've included the brand names listed in the recipe. My website is www.missimagalis.com. If you try the recipe, let me know what you think.

✳

◄9► Speaking of food … It would be a complete shame if I didn't mention the dinners at Grandma's house. I've already told you that we didn't spend the actual Christmas holiday with Grandma, and, after Mom and Dad split up, well, I am sad to say, I never saw my grandmother again.

My grandmother was a wonderful woman. She was loving and sweet and she gave the best hugs. Though I didn't see her often, I loved her very much and still do. In fact, the laptop on which I am typing at this very moment is named Gretiver after her.

In addition to being wonderful, Grandma was also a fabulous cook. Every year, close to the holidays, we'd climb in the car and take a day trip to Pennsylvania for an early holiday dinner. I always got carsick. I'd arrive at Grandma's pretty nauseous, but once I got some fresh air I was ready to eat.

Grandma had the extra-long wooden table set before we even got there. I believe there were benches, but I can't be sure. Bowls and platters of food filled the table. Grandma's mashed potatoes were my favorite.

On one occasion, I remember taking my dessert, I believe a slice of pumpkin pie, out on the back porch and enjoying it there. Every single time I read the scene in Harper Lee's *To Kill a Mockingbird* where Scout goes outside after having dinner at her aunt's house, I am reminded of sitting on the back porch after a holiday dinner at my grandma's house. The similarity between my and Scout's back porch experience ends there, but I cherish the chapter each time I read that book because it brings back the sweet memory of my grandmother. I get a clear picture of Grandma's kind smile, recall the scent of ham and turkey, the taste of her melt-in-your-mouth mashed potatoes, and I picture myself as a little girl, eating dessert on the back porch at Grandma's house while everyone else was inside. A peaceful, happy memory just for me.

※

‹8› I've been the recipient of several very special gifts, some I've mentioned already, many of which I've kept for years and years despite age and chips or tears. I love the message behind each gift, the sentimental value of the material possession. I've also been the giver of gifts, and, as you probably know, the giving feels even better than the receiving.

There's one gift I gave my mom that I absolutely love. It was a last minute gift, a poem that arrived in my mind in bits and pieces the week before Christmas. I jotted it down, reworked it until it felt right to me. It is a poem of images that remind me of my mother. I had it laminated on a strip of thick paper to serve as a bookmark. I thought I'd also include the poem here.

Before I add it, I think it's probably a good idea to mention that I have a nickname for my mother. I call her Lamuel. The name actually started out as Lammy after my niece's blanket. For some reason, after I learned that Holly had a lambskin called Lammy, I decided to start calling Mom that too. Lammy soon morphed into Lamuel, and the name stuck. It stuck so well that it's the title of my favorite gift I ever gave my mom.

Lamuel

To me, you are …

peppermint patties
blue mint dickies
brown tennis shoes

Love

Tastee-Freeze
marshmallow sundaes
good books
front porch summers

Laughter

beef tips over rice
chicken noodles
in the brown box
cruising town
my best friend

Hope

unconditional love
red toenails—glitter
spam
root beer floats

Courage

daisies-petunias

African violets

silly songs

blue eyes

cream-colored Bible

Faith

postage stamps

groceries

Holly Hobby

Nanny—Pappy

yellow-gold carpet

piano music

Friend

All my favorites …

countless wonderful

memories

Love 99

Missi

12/25/07

♥

❄

◄7► Mom is the queen of Christmas snooping. She likes to thoroughly inspect any packages that have her name on them. Her behavior is quite funny. To everyone except my brother-in-law, that is.

Mom likes everything about Christmas. She likes the decorations the shopping the wrapping the baking and especially the presents. She couldn't leave a present under the tree with her name on it if you paid her to. She's always pressing, poking, shaking, or squeezing the things. Believe me, if we ever get a fragile gift for her, we have to hide it until the big day.

Every year, for a very long time, my brother-in-law got Mom a pair of slippers. He'd wrap them up, deliver them to our house, and put them under the tree just to get Mom going. I swear she was like a cat that'd found the mother lode of catnip. As soon as the present arrived, she began quizzing him. "Can I wear it on my head? Can I take it outside? Can I hang it on the wall? Can I drink coffee out of it?" On and on the crazy questions went as she squeezed and poked the present. My brother-in-law said yes to every question.

Once he was gone, the real fun began. I'd try to keep Mom from opening the present, but I was unsuccessful. She always got into the package. For a few years, she was satisfied with opening one end and peeking to see what they looked like, but one year, the box didn't have a plastic window—it was solid cardboard, and it was taped well. My brother-in-law had caught on to her tricks and decided to make it impossible for her to see her present early.

His plan didn't work. Mom only got more courageous. This particular year, she removed all the paper, opened the cardboard box, took the slippers out, and rewrapped the box. She wore the slippers around for several days, then put them back before Christmas morning.

When my brother-in-law handed Mom the box that we knew held her slippers, she acted like she couldn't wait to tear open the package. She ripped off the paper. He laughed and said something like, "Bet ya couldn't get a peek this year, could ya?"

Mom smiled wickedly, opened the box, and pulled out the slippers. When she put them on and lifted her legs up to inspect the fabulous new slippers she was pretending to see for the first time, my brother-in-law saw that the bottoms were filthy.

"You didn't!" he exclaimed.

At first Mom didn't know what he was talking about, but when he pointed to the soles, she knew. Her face turned red, then she burst out laughing. She'd been caught, but not before Christmas. She'd successfully opened the package he'd thought she couldn't get into without destroying, paraded around in the slippers before she was even supposed to know what it was, then put them back so precisely, the package looked as perfect as the day he dropped it off. She'd have gotten away with it completely had it not been for those dirty soles. Still, she was over the moon proud of herself for the sneaky trick she almost pulled off. In fact, I believe she enjoyed getting caught, letting him know she'd won. She pranced around, gloating, having her fun.

If my memory serves me correctly, my brother-in-law was not amused. Mom didn't get slippers for the next year or two. Come to think of it, I'm not sure if she's gotten them since.

※

◄6► Christmas is still my favorite holiday after all these years. I love decorating, baking, giving gifts to those I love. And I love spending time with my family.

One of my favorite holiday celebrations is spending an evening at Dad and Betsy's. There's always all kinds of wonderful food—spiced nuts, cheese and crackers, a fruit platter, cookies, fudge, and the absolute best meatballs. In case you haven't noticed, I love food!

But, food isn't the only reason I love going there. I'm excited from the moment I get the invitation because it is a wonderful time of good conversation with people I love very much. I write the date and time on the calendar, announce it to my husband and kids, and they are always just as excited as I am.

At the end of our evening together, Dad and Betsy send home a wonderful gift of beautifully packaged baked goods. One year we received a large flour jar filled with individually wrapped treats, another year the treats were fitted into a cake platter. Last year they were piled high on a cutting board. The presentation is so beautiful, we feel a smidge guilty dismantling it. But dismantle it we do, because we can't resist what is inside—butterscotch cookies and chocolate chip, no bake goodies, and peanut butter fudge just to name a few. Then there's the rock candy. My husband always leaves with an extra bag that's just for him.

One thing is for sure, with every bite of every treat, I can taste the main ingredient that makes each so good. It isn't a secret ingredient at all. It is love.

❄

‹5› Christmas wouldn't be the same without the music. I start listening right after Halloween. My all-time favorite carol is "The First Noel." Actually, it's a tie between that and "O Holy Night." The "fall on your knees" part gets me every time.

I have another favorite too. A silly song that reminds me of my mother every single time I hear it. Until recently, I thought she was responsible for the alternate lyrics for "We Three Kings of Orient Are," but, after doing a little research, I discovered there are several versions of the cigar lyrics. I was disappointed at first. I thought Mom came up with this song just for us. But she didn't. The parody of "We Three Kings" is well known.

I thought about this for a while. How most families probably know a version of the song. And that's when it hit me. There are several *versions*, and, in all my research, I never found the one my mom sings. So, perhaps it is her very own version. Who knows? I'll tell you one thing though: once I realized that I had yet to stumble upon the one Mom sings, I quit looking. This way, I can pretend it is ours alone. To be perfectly honest, I couldn't recite the lyrics to the real "We Three Kings." I only know the silly one.

For your reading pleasure, I've written out the lyrics Mom taught me:

We three kings of Orient are
tried to smoke a rubber cigar.
It was loaded and it exploded,
and that is the end of this song.

❄

<4> Gingerbread houses. How I have struggled with the decision of whether or not I should include this story in these pages. Obviously, I decided it must be here. Of course, it is important enough. The reason I thought of omitting it is because the bitterness is so fresh that it swallows almost all of the sweet. But, I'll tell it. Because it is important. Because it is a picture of family at its best. Because it was fun. Because it was full of love.

Last Christmas my sister and her family and I along with my husband and kids all got together for a Christmas Eve dinner. It was the first time I made punch, the first time we had Christmas Eve dinner at my house, the first time we decorated gingerbread houses.

The houses were a last minute decision, something I'd thought of earlier in the week but let slip my mind because of all the other busyness during the holidays. But, on Christmas Eve, I remembered. My family and I ran to Kmart and bought four kits. When we returned, my sister and her family were at the door. I barreled up the driveway as fast as I could to explain where we'd been. I was so glad they weren't opposed to the last minute plan we'd thrown into the evening. We gathered in the kitchen and the fun began.

We split into four groups: my sister and her husband, their two daughters, my husband and I, and our three daughters. We laughed and joked, talked, decorated our houses, and helped each other. There was a little friendly competition and a sampling of the decorations as well. My goodness, did we have fun. And the houses … they were absolutely beautiful. There were candy lined windows, gumdrops around the doors, snow covered lawns and roofs, tiny balls of sugar candy that served as lights. We outdid ourselves; all four houses were grand. We lined them up on the table and took pictures, knowing that a new Christmas tradition had surely been born.

Right after Christmas, I bought four gingerbread houses from Kmart, stacked them in my closet with a satisfied smile over having a new tradition. A few days later, my niece, Holly, and I were messaging, and I told her of the purchase. She messaged me back and said she already knew. I'd told my sister, and she was excited too—so much so that she'd already told Holly the good news. Holly was just as thrilled. We messaged a few more minutes. I asked her to breakfast. She couldn't come over that morning, but said she'd love to another time. We both agreed we needed to do more together. That the gingerbread houses, the whole night actually, had been such a wonderful time …

That was the last conversation I had with my niece. She died on January 26th 2014 in a car accident. Instead of remembering that awful night, I try to keep a picture in my mind of last Christmas Eve: the smile on Holly's face, the laughter, the hugs, the love. I remind myself that she stayed at our home longer than she'd planned to that night because she was having such a good time. I miss her and I love her, and I am so sorry we didn't get the chance to keep our promise to do more together.

I hid the gingerbread houses in the back corner of the closet behind my long dresses. I can't bring myself to get rid of them, but I can't look at them anymore either.

�֎

◀3▶ When my husband and I were just starting out, times were not easy. Like many young couples, we struggled to make ends meet. Both of us worked at Skyline Caverns. I believe my husband had a second job too. I know he worked as a lifeguard in the summer, but I can't remember what he did in the fall and winter months to supplement our income. Something, I'm sure, but it was a long time ago, and I cannot bring to mind what it was. But that isn't the point.

What matters is that we were doing the best we could, and we were getting by. There were very few luxuries, and by luxuries, I mean things like paper towels. If I came home from the grocery store with a roll of these, I'd really splurged. So, I've set the stage. Times were tough, but we had a home with heat, we had clothes and hot water, and we never went hungry. And, we had the one thing that so many people crave: we had a whole lot of love.

One particular Christmas during the first years my husband and I were together stands out in my mind for one reason—because of what my mom and Bobby did for us.

My husband and I had worked all day. When we got off, we picked up our daughter from the sitter and headed home. Little did I know, Santa's elves had been hard at work. I walked into the kitchen and flipped on the light. The dining room had been transformed. A holiday tablecloth had been spread over the table; a Christmas centerpiece decorated the middle. My husband went to get a glass of tea while I opened a card Mom had left on the table. I'd barely read the message when my husband called me to the refrigerator. It was full of groceries. As was the freezer and the cabinets. We were overwhelmed with joy. Our hearts were full.

I can't recall exactly what prompted me to go upstairs, maybe a message in the card about sleeping well, or maybe I called Mom to thank her and she asked if I'd been up there. I just can't remember this part. But, prompted I was, and when I turned on the bedroom light, I pulled the classic throw-your-hand-over-your-mouth move. I really was stunned.

Our bed was covered in a brand new comforter, cream with pink roses, and shams to match. On the windows were matching curtains. I jumped onto the bed, feeling just like a princess.

I'm sure I called my mother back, or ran down to her house (We lived on the same street.), or yelled with joy, or laughed out loud. I probably did all of these things. I know my husband and I thanked Mom and Bobby again and again. We were both so grateful.

That year, giving us a kitchen full of food and a bedroom makeover was the highlight of Mom and Bobby's Christmas. They were just so happy to give.

Thank you again and again for such a wonderfully thoughtful gift.

✻

◄2► Some holiday traditions begin when you get married, others when you start a family. Others still are traditions that have been passed down through the years from your parents and their parents and generations before.

My husband and I started the Christmas pickle after we'd had all three of our daughters, but they were all still pretty young. If our daughters have children, I think they'll have a Christmas pickle too. Every year we also leave the television on TBS for the entire twenty-four hours that *A Christmas Story* plays. These are just a couple of the traditions we've sprinkled in among others that were given to us as gifts from our parents when we were very young.

My husband and I carried on the tradition of stockings, of course. Leaving cookies and milk for Santa is another one. We drive around Front Royal to look at all the beautiful lights. Our Main Street has to be the most fabulous Main Street of all the Main Streets in the world. The wreaths on the lamp posts, the decorations in the store windows—what an amazing sight. It is breathtaking, really. Last year, one store had an upside down tree that hung from the ceiling. It was awesome.

Like my parents, my husband and I also let the kids open one present on Christmas Eve. So far, they've gotten pajamas every single year, even though I promise they are getting something other than sleepwear. They've told me it would be weird to get anything other than pajamas on Christmas Eve, that I can try and fool them, but to please not change a thing. The girls are so attached to this tradition, I am certain we've sealed the deal—their children will receive a lifetime of Christmas Eve pajamas as well.

The food. Goodness me, the food. That's a tradition I could never let go. I love to bake cookies and try new holiday recipes. I love to name the Christmas turkey (the Thanksgiving one too). My husband and I brine the bird. The sweet and savory scents of holiday feasts bring my heart such peace and joy.

I'm grateful my parents and grandparents blessed my life with family traditions that will forever live in my heart.

❮1❯

Dear Mom and Dad,

Thank you for having me, for raising me the best way you knew how, for giving me the childhood that helped shape me into the person I am today.

Thank you for the memories, both good and bad, though I have to say that, no matter how bad the worst got, the good memories, they shine like the brightest stars in the planet.

I am blessed to have you as parents, blessed to have two stepparents who love me for who I am, blessed to have family traditions that you began so that I would have something to take with me and share with my own family.

This book is a gift to you both that I hope will serve as a final healing of any regret or shame or bitterness left over from mistakes that you feel you haven't paid dearly enough for yet. We are human. We all make mistakes. Some more devastating than others, some that inflict wounds that remain open and sore for a very long time. Just when you think they're finally beginning to heal, something happens, and the wounds bleed again. If this is true for you as it has been for me, my prayer is that you might read in these pages all the good you gave me, all the sweet loving memories for which I am so grateful, and know that these kernels of goodness are what I remember most vividly. You gave more than your best. I feel very blessed.

Merry Christmas, Mom and Dad.

I love you,

Missi

Photo Credit: Brooke Magalis

**Missi Magalis** is the author of *Merry Christmas, Mom and Dad, Good Morning, Mrs. Clark, Beautifully Broken, How Do You Do, Mrs. Wiley?,* and *Ashmikisle Out of the Ashes.* She was born and raised in Front Royal, Virginia, and earned degrees from Lord Fairfax Community College and Shenandoah University. She resides in her hometown with her husband and three daughters. Visit her website at www.missimagalis.com.

36094401R00037

Made in the USA
Charleston, SC
25 November 2014